Tracks

Written by Rob Morrison

INTRODUCTION

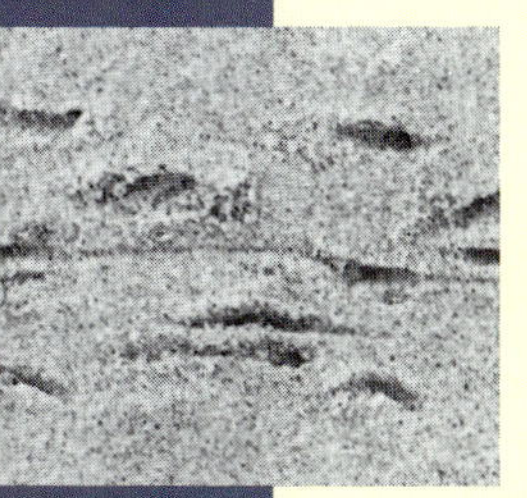

People usually work and play during the daytime, but many animals are most active at night.

In warm climates the daytime may be too hot for some animals, so they often feed and travel at night, when it is cooler.

For many small animals the daytime may be too dangerous, so they, too, are active at night, because the darkness hides them.

It is possible to walk through the countryside in the daytime and be surrounded by animals that you never see.

You would not even know they were there—if it were not for the signs that they leave behind.

Signs left by animals may be their droppings, scratchings on a
tree trunk, nests, partly eaten food, holes that they have dug,
and the footprints and tracks that they leave as they walk,
hop, run, or gallop.

This drawing shows the actual size of the shell. The artist has
placed it alongside the tracks, in each photograph. It will give
you an idea of the size of the footprints and their distance
apart.

The animal that made this track:

- has four feet

- can walk, run, and gallop

- is 3 feet long

What animal is it?

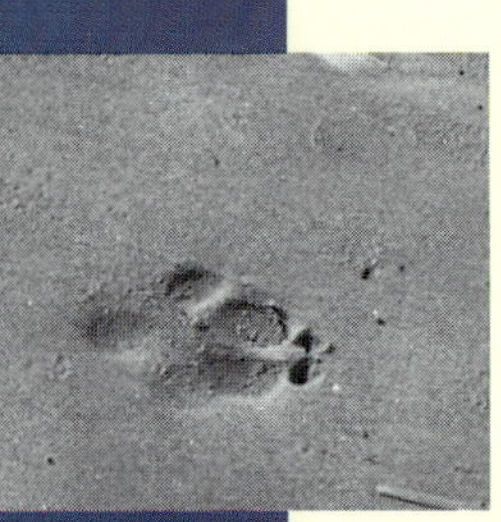

A DOG

- Dogs are mammals.

- A dog's forefeet are slightly larger than its hindfeet, and they make a larger print in its tracks.

- A dog's track can tell you how fast it was running, because the faster it runs, the farther apart its footprints will be.

- A dog's track shows the marks of the strong claws that it uses to dig with when it buries bones.

The animal that made this track:

- has four feet

- steps on top of its own footprints

- is 16 inches long

What animal is it?

A CAT

- Cats are mammals.

- When cats walk, they place their hindfeet on top of the prints of their forefeet. This helps them move silently when they go hunting.

- Because cats can withdraw their claws, these do not leave any mark in a cat's track.

- Cat tracks sometimes show where they have buried their droppings.

The animal that made this track:

- swims much better than it can walk

- has flippers instead of legs

- is 7½ feet long

What animal is it?

A SEA LION

- A sea lion is also a mammal, but its body is better adapted to swimming than walking.

- When a sea lion is in the sea, water supports its body. On land, its body drags on the ground and leaves a wide track, when it moves.

- A sea lion uses its flippers to push itself through the sand. Its body is so heavy that the flippers dig deep holes.

- A sea lion is like a seal, but it has small ear flaps on the side of its head. You cannot see a true seal's ears, and a seal spends less time on land than a sea lion does.

The animal that made this track:

- has large feet that leave big footprints

- has two toes on each foot

- is 9½ feet long

What animal is it?

A CAMEL

- Camels are mammals.

- An Arabian camel has one hump, and a Bactrian camel has two. Arabian camels are sometimes called dromedaries.

- A camel's feet are large and flat, to stop it from sinking into the sand.

- Arabian camels can travel long distances without drinking. They are useful animals in the desert.

The animal that made this track:

- has six feet

- moves its legs in a very regular pattern

- is 1 inch long

What animal is it?

A BEETLE

- Beetles are insects, and adult insects have six legs.

- They move their legs in a very regular pattern, so that they do not trip themselves up.

- They have many sharp claws on their feet, so that they can cling to the bark and leaves of trees.

The animal that made this track:

- has ten legs

- moves in an unusual way

- is 4 inches long

What animal is it?

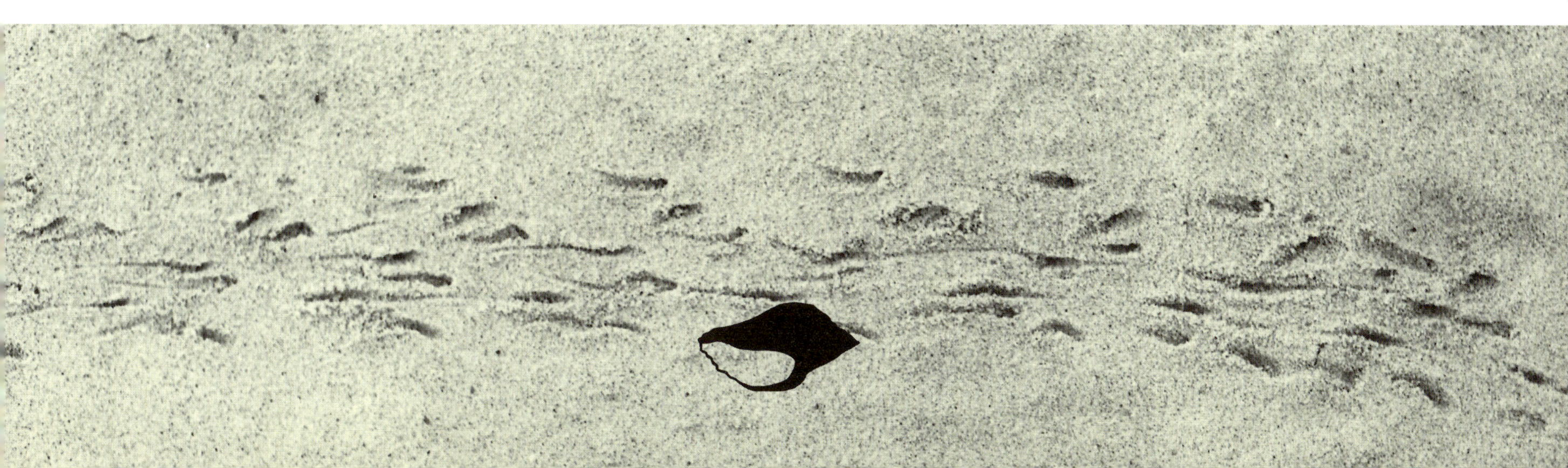

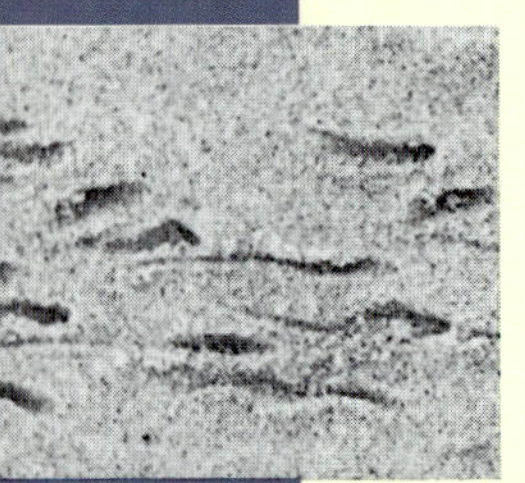

A CRAB

- Crabs belong to a group of animals called crustaceans.

- Crabs walk sideways.

- Most crustaceans have ten legs, but some, such as shrimps and prawns, use their legs more for swimming than for walking.

The animal that made this track:

- has two feet

- has webs between its toes

- is 14 inches long

What animal is it?

A GULL

- Gulls are birds. Most birds, like the gull, leave footprints that show the marks of three toes.

- Each foot has a fourth toe that points backward. It is too high up on the leg to leave its mark in footprints.

- The small webs between a gull's toes help it to swim.

The animal that made this track:

- has four feet

- makes a track with its body as well as its feet

- is 9 inches long

What animal is it?

A TORTOISE

- Tortoises are reptiles. Like many other reptiles, tortoises drag their bodies along the ground.

- A tortoise's body is encased in a shell that scrapes a wide track between the footprints.

- A tortoise has a small pointed tail that makes a narrow groove down the middle of the track.

The animal that made this track:

- drags its body along the ground

- leaves no footprints because it has no legs

- is 2½ feet long

What animal is it?

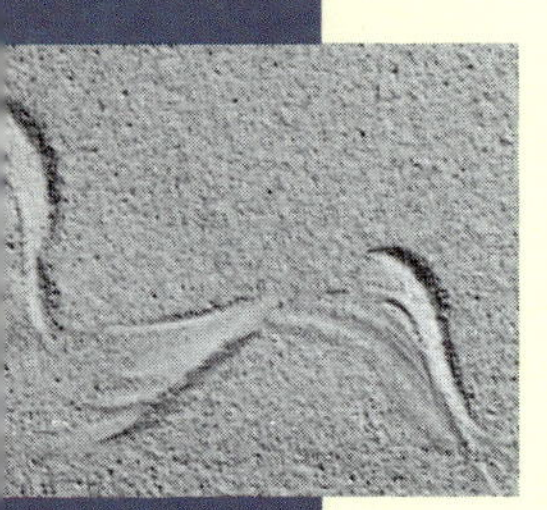

A SNAKE

- Snakes are reptiles. Like many other snakes, this one moves by wriggling from side to side.

- The curves of the snake's body make small hills of dirt behind it, and it pushes against the small hills to move itself forward.

- Snake tracks may be hard to find during winter. The weather and the ground may become too cold for the snakes, so they hide away until it is spring.

GLOSSARY

adapted	adjusted or changed to suit a particular purpose
Arabian camel	a camel that has one hump on its back
Bactrian camel	a camel that has two humps on its back
crustaceans	a group of animals, most of which live in water, and have a hard body covering; for example, crabs, shrimps, and lobsters
dromedary	another name for an Arabian camel
mammals	a group of animals that have warm blood, hair, and feed their young with milk
reptiles	a group of cold-blooded animals, such as snakes, and lizards, that have water-proof skins and lay eggs

INDEX